MORE · 1 · IDEAS

by Edward
Ramsbottom

Illustrated
by
Margaret
Sutton

Acknowledgements

The author and publishers wish to thank the following, who have kindly given permission for the use of copyright material: Brockhampton Press Ltd for the extract from *Malay Schooner* by Clive Dalton; Christopher Busby & John Rose Ltd for 'Long Distance Lorry' by Philip Callow; Jonathan Cape Ltd and the Executrix of the Arthur Ransome Estate for extracts from *Pigeon Post* and *Winter Holiday* by Arthur Ransome; Daily Mirror for 'Anger' by Yvonne Karen Lowe, reproduced by kind permission of the Daily Mirror Children's Literary Competition; Harcourt Brace Jovanovich, Inc. for 'Fog' from *Chicago Poems* by Carl Sandburg, copyright 1914 by Holt, Rinehart & Winston Inc., renewed 1942 by Carl Sandburg; William Heinemann Ltd for 'The Wind' from *The Wandering Moon* by James Reeves.

The publishers have made every effort to trace the copyright-holders, but if they have inadvertently overlooked any, they will be pleased to make the necessary arrangement at the first opportunity.

The publishers wish to acknowledge the following sources of photographs: Jacques Penry, Facial Topographer, p. 18; Popperfoto Library, p. 16; The National Gallery, p. 41.

First published 1974

Published by
MACMILLAN EDUCATION LTD
London and Basingstoke

Associated companies and representatives
throughout the world

Designed by First Impressions, Basingstoke
Filmset by BAS Printers Limited, Wallop, Hampshire
Printed photolitho in Great Britain by
Ebenezer Baylis and Son Limited
The Trinity Press, Worcester, and London

Out of One Mind into Another

Read the sentence below. Think what it means and discuss it with your friends.

> *The final cause of speech and writing is to get an idea, as exactly as possible, out of one mind into another.*
>
> G. M. Young

You may ask, "What is the best way to get an idea, as exactly as possible, out of my mind and into someone else's?"

Here is some advice which may help you when you speak and write:

1 **Think until the idea is clear in your mind.**
2 **Choose plain, simple words.**
3 **Say what you mean in as few words as possible.**

Try it Yourself

Think of someone or something at home that none of your friends has seen. Then describe the person or article to them as clearly as you can.

Here are some suggestions:

My most treasured possession
My dad (in a good mood, or when he gets annoyed)
My bedroom
Our car

Making a Plan

Before you start to write (and sometimes before you speak), it is useful to jot down notes as they come to your mind. You can then take this a stage further and sort out your rough notes into a plan.

What is the first thing you remember in your life? As you think, jot down notes of everything you recall about that event. Sort out your notes into a plan and then write an account of your earliest memory.

Writing a Story

Here is a very simple story written by a six-year-old girl who had just started to learn how to write about her own thoughts:

> I am a mouse and I live in a hole. I would like a house. I have adventures. Once I went to a witch's house and stole some gold and silver. Then I went home. I was rich.

Imagine you are a mouse or any other small creature. Make notes of your thoughts and feelings. Then sort your notes into a plan and use the plan to help you to write a story. Susan pretended she was a hedgehog. Here are the notes she made:

1 all prickles and spines
2 living in the hedgerows
3 food—snails, worms, slugs
4 adventure in a garden—dog barking
5 frightened—a tight ball of prickles
6 how I escaped.

Now start to plan your story.

Poetry

A poet has his own thoughts and feelings about life. He takes great care to choose the right words to express what he thinks and feels in his poetry.

Fog

Have you ever walked through fog? Perhaps you felt the cold, clammy fog fold around you like a thin, soft blanket. Read these lines by Carl Sandburg. He describes fog as he sees it.

> *The fog comes*
> *on little cat feet.*
>
> *It sits looking*
> *over the harbour and city*
> *on silent haunches*
> *and then moves on.*

Read the verse again. Notice that there are no rhymes.

Discuss with your friends the ideas and feelings that come to your mind when you think of fog. Write down words, phrases and ideas that come from the discussion. Here are notes made by one group of friends:

quiet stillness
ghostly shapes
moisture on a woollen scarf
smoke and fog—smog

After your discussion write a verse or two or three sentences about fog.

Wind

I can get through a doorway without any key,
And strip the leaves from the great oak tree.
I can drive storm-clouds and shake tall towers,
Or steal through a garden and not wake the flowers.
Seas I can move and ships I can sink;
I can carry a house-top or the scent of a pink.
When I am angry I can rave and riot;
And when I am spent, I lie quiet as quiet.

In this poem James Reeves imagines himself to be the wind. In a very few words he tells of some of the things he can do and of his different moods: sometimes he is strong, rough and powerful; sometimes gentle and quiet.

Clouds

Here are notes about clouds, written by people of about your age. Notice how they used their imagination to describe what they saw.

yachts with full sails
sky ships sailing
light, fluffy cotton wool
dark, grey blanket

Make notes of your own about one of the following:

clouds   **rain**
the sun   **the sky**

Now write several sentences, or a verse, using the notes you have made.

Listen

There are many other words and phrases that are frequently used instead of the correct words. Listen for these words and phrases in conversation and on television: 'you see', 'sort of', 'kind of', 'who's it', 'er . . .', 'er . . . like', 'thing-ummy', 'what's its name', 'if you understand'.

Avoid using these words yourself, and think before you speak so that you always say what you mean.

The Right Words

People who do not take the trouble to choose the right words when they talk often use such words as 'you know' at the end of each phrase or sentence. Other people sometimes add a little more, but leave you to sort out exactly what they mean. They say, ". . . if you know what I mean", or ". . . or something like that".

If you take care to choose the right words to express your thoughts, there is a much better chance that people will understand what you do mean.

Try to be Accurate

If you are going to choose the right words to express what is in your mind, you must first be sure about the meanings of words you would like to use.

You can find out about words in three ways:

1 by guessing their meanings from how they are used in speech and in what you read
2 by asking someone to explain their meanings to you
3 by looking up the words in a dictionary.

We get the feel of what words mean from how other people use them. In reading we often guess the meaning of a 'new' word from the sense of the words around it. Try to remember and use new words that you see and hear.

The Word Detective

John always listened and looked for words that were new to him. One day his father told the family of an incident he saw on his way home from work.

He said, "I didn't know what to do. I was in a real dilemma. I didn't know whether to run after the thief or try to catch his mate, who had slipped on the pavement."

Later John said, "I think I know what 'dilemma' means."

What do you think 'dilemma' means?

Can you think of a time when you were in a dilemma? Write about it, or tell a short story about someone else who was in a dilemma.

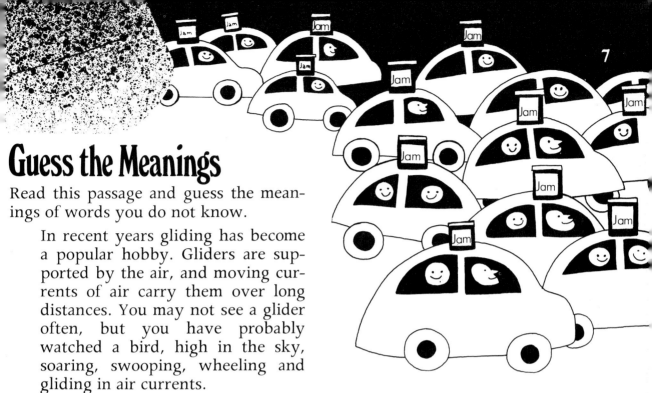

Guess the Meanings

Read this passage and guess the meanings of words you do not know.

> In recent years gliding has become a popular hobby. Gliders are supported by the air, and moving currents of air carry them over long distances. You may not see a glider often, but you have probably watched a bird, high in the sky, soaring, swooping, wheeling and gliding in air currents.

Different Meanings

In the passage about gliding, the word 'supported' is used in the sense that air 'supports' or 'holds up' the gliders. But the word 'support' can also be used in the sense that parents 'support' or 'provide for' a family.

When you hear or read a word, you should always try to find out the sense in which it is being used.

Here are some words that you know:

> lace   note   place   plain   bear

Can you think of more than one meaning for each word? For example:

> You 'catch' a ball.
> A question may have a 'catch'.
> A fisherman has a good 'catch'.

Now find other words of this kind.

Unexpected Meanings

Some words and phrases have unexpected meanings that can alter the sense of what people are trying to say.

Make drawings to illustrate ambiguous phrases that you have come across. Show that you can see more than one meaning for each phrase. Do any of the following ideas appeal to you?

> traffic jam
> a wrestling match
> a walking stick
> hitting the nail on the head
> striking while the iron is hot
> turning over a page
> running a temperature
> a skeleton key
> drawing water

Codes and Dictionaries

Codes are often used to send secret messages.

This is a very simple message in code:

It is meaningless until you know the key to the code that has been used.

In this code J stands for A, K for B and so on.

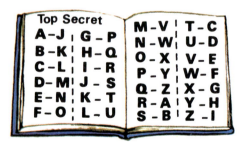

So the message reads:

FN   JCCJ LT   JC   MJ FW
WE   ATTACK   AT   DAWN

Make up a message, and use this code to send it to a friend. Let him use the key to decode the message.

A Code of Your Own

Write out the alphabet and give each letter a different symbol. Then send another message in code to your friend and ask him to read it, using the key.

Dictionaries

There are other kinds of codes. Many codes use ordinary words, but give them special meanings only known to people who have the key.

When you read a passage which contains a lot of words that you do not know, it is sometimes similar to trying to read a message in code without the key. But you can use a dictionary to find out the meanings of new words. Make a habit of using a dictionary to 'decode' words you do not know.

Using a Dictionary

The words in a dictionary are arranged in alphabetical order. To find a word, you must be sure of its spelling, or at least of what its first three or four letters are.

Look at the words in **bold** type at the top of a page. In most dictionaries there are two such index words at the top of each page. These are the first and last words listed on that page. You will notice that, like the other words, they are arranged alphabetically.

By glancing at the index words, you can quickly find the pages which deal with the letter of the alphabet that you need.

Look again at the word you are trying to find. Now search for the index word which is the closest to it, with the second, third, and perhaps even fourth letters the same as your word. Look down the words on that page until you find the one that you are searching for.

SPIDER LAUGH room WORK stamp Yes GUIDE bumpe ear EASTER SATURDAY secret pen NATIONAL Romar excellence

NEW YORK

Dictionary Practice

Spend a few moments practising how to use a dictionary quickly and properly.

Find the beginnings of the sections which start with these letters:

K   D   W   B   J   E   N

Write down the first word in each of these sections and read its meaning. (Not all dictionaries begin a particular section with the same word.)

Find the last words listed in the sections beginning with:

S   A   L   O   Y   P   T

and read how the dictionary defines each one.

Find these words in your dictionary and see if you can discover how they are connected with each other:

wages   payment   cash   remittance   salary

The First to Find

With a group of friends, have a competition to see who is the first to find each of the words that are listed below. Start with your dictionaries closed. At a signal, find the word as quickly as possible and read out what is written about it.

Here are the words:

foreign	brittle	siege
descend	increase	decision
menagerie	riot	equator

Alphabetical Order

Words, names and lists are often arranged in alphabetical order. This makes it a simple matter to find any particular word or item. Think of places where words, names or lists are arranged in alphabetical order.

Telephone Directories

Ask your teacher if you may use a telephone directory, and find the telephone numbers of:

your doctor, dentist, or school
a local shop where your family buys food
a friend or relative who lives in your district
a garage near to school (from the 'yellow pages')

Think of other people whose telephone numbers you could find, and make a small directory of your own.

How would you obtain the number of someone living in a town in another part of the country?

Indexes

An index is a list, arranged in alphabetical order, of important names or items mentioned in a book. At the side of each name in the list is printed the number of the page or pages where the name is mentioned. An index can be found at the back of most reference books.

Find a book with an index. Turn to the index and choose a subject that interests you. Use the index to find the information given in the book and then make notes of some of the facts you have learned.

If you wish to take the idea further, you can make a topic of the subject and collect more information from other reference books. In your search you will find it useful to know how to use an index.

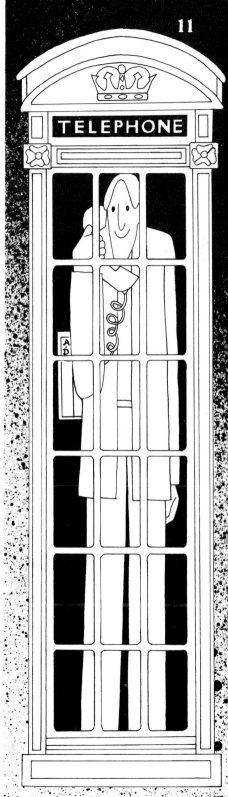

Nouns

From where you are sitting, look around and name twenty things that you can see. Tell them to a group of friends or write them as a list. You might begin with:

wall   floor   desk

If you have named them correctly, you will have said or written twenty nouns. A noun is the name of a person, a creature, an idea or a thing.

Through the Alphabet

Play this game with a group of friends. Each person in turn says a noun beginning with 'a', then one beginning with 'b' and so on through the alphabet. The simplest way to score is to count a point for each letter that is missed. The person with the lowest score is the winner.

Name by Touch

Place twenty or thirty objects in a bag. Small articles, such as a thimble, a coin or a rubber, are suitable for this experiment. With eyes closed, feel in the bag and take out one object at a time. Name it. The word you use will be a noun—the name of the object in your hand.

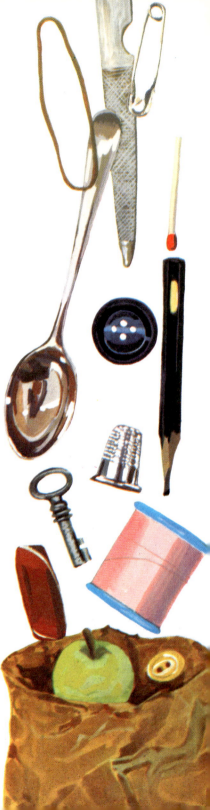

Adjectives

Words that describe nouns are called 'adjectives'. You can choose suitable adjectives to describe people, creatures and things by using your five senses. This means that you can describe things as they appear to you.

Much of what you think and feel about people, places and events in your life comes from what you discover by using your five senses. The notes below suggest ways in which you can use your senses to explore the world.

SIGHT

From observation of people and things, you can describe the colour, shape, size, pattern and movement of everything you see.

HEARING

By listening carefully, you can describe the volume, quality and type of each sound you hear.

TOUCH

By feeling, you can tell the roughness, smoothness, hardness, softness, shape, weight and temperature of everything you touch.

SMELL

Scents and smells often remind people of places and events. They can give pleasure or warn of danger.

TASTE

The taste buds of your tongue can identify four basic tastes: salt, sweet, bitter and sour.

Using Your Senses

Collect several objects. Find some which have a special shape, colour, size or texture, others which have a distinctive taste or smell and others which make a particular sound.

Examine each object carefully (through a magnifying glass if you can find one). Use your senses to discover everything you can about each one.

Now choose suitable words to describe each object. Make a display of the objects on a tray or table, and label each item with the adjectives you have chosen.

One group of children labelled their items:

sharp, shiny (a new pin)
rough, jagged (a broken brick)
soft, smooth (velvet)

Mystery and Adventure

In the poem, 'Flannan Isle', W. W. Gibson tells an interesting story in which three lighthouse-men mysteriously disappear, leaving no sign of what has happened to them.

Exciting mysteries very rarely happen in everyday life, but you could write a mystery story of your own. Imagine that you were on your way to a friend's house, just as it was getting dark. He was expecting you. When you arrived at the house, all the lights were on and the door was open. You knocked, but no one answered.

Write a story describing:

1 your journey to the house
2 the house
3 what you found
4 what you did.

Down a Mine

Perhaps you like to read adventure stories. Some of these stories are set on lonely islands, in far-off lands, in aeroplanes, or in places where many people have never been. Here is a short extract from *Pigeon Post*, by Arthur Ransome:

> A new noise sounded close by, a deep, hollow rumbling and clattering like a goods wagon banging over the points in a railway siding. A light suddenly appeared and a small loaded trolley swung round out of a side tunnel and rattled away ahead with a man trotting behind it.

The book tells of an adventure four children had in this dark mine.

Try to remember a time when you were in a dark place. Were you afraid? Could you see, hear, smell or feel anything? What happened? Write about it.

In the Air

Imagine you could fly like a bird for one hour. Think how you would feel as you swooped and soared in the sky.

Write the story of your adventures. Choose the words you use carefully.

Clothes and People

Read these lines of verse by Elizabeth Jennings:

My mother keeps on telling me
When she was in her teens
She wore quite different clothes from mine
And hadn't heard of jeans,

T-shirts, no hats, and dresses that
Reach far above our knees.
I laughed at first and then I thought
One day my kids will tease

And scoff at what I'm wearing now.
What will their fashions be?
I'd give an awful lot to know,
To look ahead and see.

Girls dressed like girls perhaps once more
And boys no longer half
Resembling us. Oh, what's in store
To make our children laugh?

Discussion

With your friends, talk about:

clothes you like wearing
your personal appearance
(your height, build,
complexion, eyes and hair)
fashions you do not like

Mime a Job

Think of the job your father does and then do a mime to show his work. If the job is too difficult to mime, think of some other kind of work. Ask your friends to guess your mime and to describe the kind of clothes a person doing the job would wear.

Special Clothes

Collect and draw pictures of people who wear special clothes for their work. Make a folder or frieze of them.

Choose one picture and make notes about it, naming the various parts of the clothing. Mention as many details as you can. If possible, choose someone whom you see often and can look at carefully.

Here are two suggestions:

the school caretaker
a lady who serves school meals

A Story

Plan a story which begins with a description of the person you have made notes about. For example, if you were using a description of a guardsman to begin your story, you could imagine him on guard at the entrance to an important building, and make a plan like this:

1 the guardsman
2 where he was—time of day
3 crowds of sightseers
4 the royal coach arriving
5 salute by the guard
6 his feelings as he watched the crowds slowly disappear.

Now make your plan and write the story of an incident which happened to the person you have chosen.

Full Description, Please

When policemen investigate a crime, they often ask witnesses for descriptions of people suspected of committing the crime. If the crime is serious, these descriptions are sent by radio to police stations throughout the country.

The police also take descriptions of people who are missing.

Think of someone you know well, either at school or at home. Imagine that he is a 'missing person' and that you have to give a full description of him to the police. Make notes and then write the description, giving as much information as you can. The police will ask you how old the person is. Can you judge a person's age (to within a few years)?

Can other people who know the person guess who it is from your description?

Suspicious Behaviour

Imagine you were hiding in a secret spot near your home. Suddenly you saw someone acting suspiciously. You held your breath, kept quite still and watched. Note down what happened, in the form of a plan, before writing a full account of what you saw.

Here is the plan that Michael made:

1 my secret hide-out
2 sound of someone approaching
3 his appearance—my suspicions
4 digging—what happened
5 what I did.

Shades of Meaning

Look at these words:

old   aged   ancient   antique

You probably know them and realise that each one is connected with age. 'Old' is the simplest of the words and can be used widely—an old building, an old trick and so on. The other three words have different shades of meaning. Look up each one in your dictionary. (A good dictionary will give examples to show how each word may be used.)

With your friends, discuss how to use each of the words. To start the discussion, decide what is wrong with this sentence:

An antique man looked in an aged magazine for details about old furniture.

A Story

Draw up a plan for a story, based on one of these suggestions:

finding something very old in your home (a key, a ring, a brooch, a newspaper cutting or, perhaps, a lock of hair)

the oldest person you know

a visit to a museum or an old building, such as a castle

Size

Think about each of the words below. Decide on the different shades of meaning between them and the different senses in which they can be used.

1 **little   small   tiny   mini   microscopic   minute**

2 **big   huge   large   gross   gigantic   maxi   enormous**

'Mini' and 'maxi' are used as words by many people, but they are really only parts of words. Use a dictionary to find words beginning with 'mini' and 'maxi'.

A Change in Size

What would your world be like if you were an insect?
Here are two ideas to think about:

Imagine you are a tiny fly on a wall in your home at teatime. Describe the scene from your new point of view. What do you hear and see? What happens?

Imagine you are a wasp buzzing round a garden where a fat, old gentleman is dozing off to sleep. Write a story about your thoughts, and about what happens.

More Shades of Meaning

Look at these words and find their meanings:

extinguish   eject

It may help if you think of a fire extinguisher, and an ejector seat in an aeroplane.

One boy asked his father the meaning of these words and was told they meant 'put out'. Later the boy wrote this sentence:

Last night my father ejected the light and extinguished the cat.

What did he mean to say?

With your friends, discuss the following two sentences and say what each of them means.

I can hear you, but I'm not listening.
I'm listening, but I can't hear you.

Imagine situations in which these sentences might be used. Discuss them and then write several sentences or a short story based on the ideas you have thought of.

Tones of Voice

We often give a clearer meaning to the words we use by our tone of voice. You can prove this by talking to a pet dog. If you say to the dog, "Bad dog, bad dog," in a gentle and kind voice, he will wag his tail and show he is pleased. But if you shout angrily and harshly, "Good dog, you're a very good dog," he will lower his tail and think he's done something wrong.

Think about the different tones of voice you would use if you were:

**angry   sleepy   miserable
polite   pleased   pleading**

Now act the following situations, using your own words and your tone of voice to make your feelings clear.

> You are asking your mother if you can go out with two friends next Saturday afternoon.
>
> You have woken up late, feeling very warm and sleepy, and your mother has just told you for the third time to get up.
>
> It is your birthday and you have just been given the very thing you wanted most.

Choose one of the incidents and write out the story as clearly as you can.

The Human Voice

Think about the different sounds you can make with your voice. Now make a list of words which express the ways in which you use your voice. Begin with:

whisper   speak   shout

When you have made your list, choose one kind of sound and make it the starting-point of a story. It could be any sound made by the human voice.

Here are some ideas:

> **As I quietly opened the kitchen door, a roar of hearty laughter met me . . .**
>
> **I heard a low, hooting sound—a secret signal known only to my friends and myself . . .**

Expressing Yourself

We have seen that there are various ways of expressing yourself. We have considered:

1 **the idea in your mind**
2 **the words you choose to say what you mean**
3 **your tone of voice**

but other important ways of conveying what you feel are by the expressions on your face and the gestures you make with your hands, and by other body movements.

Expressions & Gestures

Think about the situations below and then act each of them, using suitable gestures and expressions.

You are on your own in a strange town and you want to find a café for a meal. You stop a passer-by and ask him the way to the nearest café. He is very kind and wants to help, but you discover that he is deaf.

You meet a friend in the street and stop to talk. Your friend has a young puppy. You pet it and then continue talking. The puppy gets impatient, jumps up at you and finally starts to snap and bite at your shoes.

Work with a partner. Imagine that one is the parent and the other is the child. The child has just come home with his clothes badly torn.

Now choose one of the incidents and write out a description of what happened. Don't forget the gestures and expressions that were used and the people's thoughts and feelings.

Movements

Make a list of words which express actions, movements and gestures made by people, or by animals. You might begin with these:

| crawl | scramble | shuffle |
| shrug | stamp | creep |

Choose an action, movement or gesture as the starting-point of a story. Here is one possible starting-point:

I was tingling with excitement as I wandered into the huge, empty warehouse. All my senses were suddenly very keen and alert. A soft, scratching, scampering sound came from the right and I froze in horror as a huge rat shuffled across the floor just in front of me, and disappeared under a pile of rubbish and old boxes in a corner.

VERBS

With your friends, say as many verbs (words that express actions) as you can in one minute. If you want to make it a competition, you can each write down as many verbs as possible in one minute. Here are three to begin with:

run   throw   kick

Now discuss the following words with your friends and try to decide why they are verbs.

**think   look   decide   guess
try   possess   risk   see**

Compose a different sentence for each of the verbs. Then write a story beginning with a sentence such as:

**I decided to go ahead with my plan.
I will risk the consequences.**

Mimimg Verbs

In your group, take turns at miming these verbs:

hop   stretch   kneel   bend   lift

Now make it into a game. One person thinks of a verb and mimes it. The others try to guess the verb. The first person to guess correctly scores a point and is the next to choose a verb.

Sentences

Expressing what you feel in a lively, vigorous way is perhaps the most important part of speaking and writing. But it is also important that people who read what you have written should understand it without difficulty. To make it easy to follow the ideas in a piece of writing, we write in sentences.

A sentence always begins with a capital letter and ends with a full stop. Between the capital letter and the full stop are words which have been put together to express an idea. Every sentence must have at least one verb.

Ideas into Sentences

Look at the children in the picture below. Each of them has had an idea, but has not said anything about it to anyone.

Choose one of the ideas and write what you think the boy or girl would say to express it clearly in words. You might write one or several sentences.

Now think of ideas of your own and write sentences to express each idea.

Verbs in Sentences

Read the sentences below and pick out the verbs. Remember that a verb expresses an action.

John threw the ball at the wicket.

In the dim light a shadowy figure crept towards the house.

The children jumped, danced and clapped as they cheered the clowns in the circus.

Sentence Game

Play this sentence game in a group. Each person should say a verb in turn and the others in the group should then compose sentences using that verb.

This is how one group started:

Nigel: The verb is 'push'.
Mary: Sometimes when we go shopping I push the pram, but I never cross the street with the pram.

Stages of a Story

It is important that the sentences that you write should follow each other in an orderly way and tell the story clearly. To be sure that your story is clearly told, always go through the following stages when you write:

1 Think of an idea.
2 Jot down notes of the main points of the story.
3 Go through your notes and make a plan.
4 Write your story in sentences.

Choose one of the titles below and make a plan for a story. Then write the story in full.

My journey to school
If I could please myself
A time when I was very afraid
When I felt shy
Ill in bed
A surprise I shall never forget

Checking Your Writing

It is easy to say, "write in sentences", but it is sometimes difficult for young people to know whether what they have written is a sentence.

The best way to check this is to read through your work and see if what you have written as a sentence makes sense. A capital letter and a full stop indicate the beginning and end of a sentence, but the sentence that lies between them should consist of a complete idea which makes sense when it is read with the other sentences that are used with it.

Check your writing by reading it through and looking at each sentence in turn.

Which of these are sentences?

Along the street the little boy. In the distance a police car appeared. With a flashing light on the roof. The little boy near the accident. Soon the ambulance arrived.

Write out this account in sentences.

What Do You Mean?

It is surprising what fun you can have if you listen closely to what people say, and read carefully what they write.

Some people have a clear idea of what they want to say. They choose the right words, but they end up by saying or writing something they did not mean.

Read these sentences and advertisements. Think what they mean and what they were intended to mean.

> Mary went home wearing a coat with her friend.
>
> There was a discussion yesterday about sheep worrying in the village hotel.
>
> WANTED oak table by old lady with carved and twisted legs.
>
> WANTED young waitress, must be clean until July.
>
> The door opened and a young woman carrying a baby and her husband entered.
>
> As the procession passed, he stood on the balcony and threw streamers with his friends.
>
> I know a man with a wooden leg called Long John.

With your friends, discuss each of the sentences and advertisements. Say:

1 what each sentence or advertisement means
2 what it was intended to mean
3 why the order in which words are placed is important.

SLOW POLICE

Notice on the wooden sign: **OVEN READY CHICKENS AND PONIES FOR SALE**

Notices

There are some notices in the pictures above. They may make you smile, but think what they mean and what they were intended to mean.

How would you write these signs?

Collecting Slips

Notice any slips or mistakes that are made in the newspapers and magazines that you read. Many of these errors will make you smile. Bring cuttings of them to school and display them on a frieze.

Misunderstandings

A young boy was always given the job of fetching the evening newspaper from a nearby shop. He liked to do it as quickly as he could and was always trying to beat his record time. One evening his father gave him fifty pence and said that he could keep the money that he had when he got home if he beat his record time to the shop and back.

The boy arrived home breathless in a few minutes, having broken his record —but without the paper! His father decided to let him keep the fifty pence.

Write about a misunderstanding or mix-up which happened in your family.

Different Kinds of Constructions

Have you ever wondered about the construction of buildings in your town? Builders use various basic materials—bricks, cement, steel, wood, glass and other substances—and from them they construct many different buildings.

Read these lines:

Houses huddle together and spires
Of towering flats rise above squat
And sprawling factories, offices and shops;
An interlocked mass of bricks, cement and steel.
Looping patterns of ribboned roads,
Busy with fuming traffic, thread through
Linking home and work within the city.

Does the town where you live have an interesting variety of buildings in its landscape? Draw a picture of buildings and roads near your home.

Homes

With your friends, discuss the area around your home. Here are ideas to start your discussion:

where you live (house or flat)
buildings nearby (tall, ugly, old, modern)
special buildings or landmarks
colour, noise, movement of traffic and people
thoughts and feelings about where you live

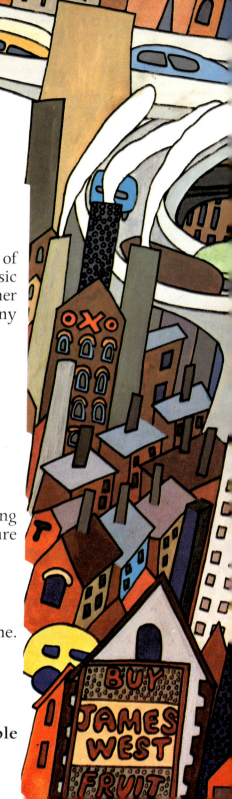

Different Kinds of Sentences

When you write a story, do you give much thought to making the sentences interesting? Even the most exciting story loses some of its sparkle if every sentence begins in the same way.

Just as an architect varies the construction of his buildings by using materials in different ways, so a good writer varies the construction of his sentences by using words in different orders. But an architect must keep to certain rules, and so must a writer. Can you list some of the rules a writer must follow?

Try to vary the construction of your sentences.

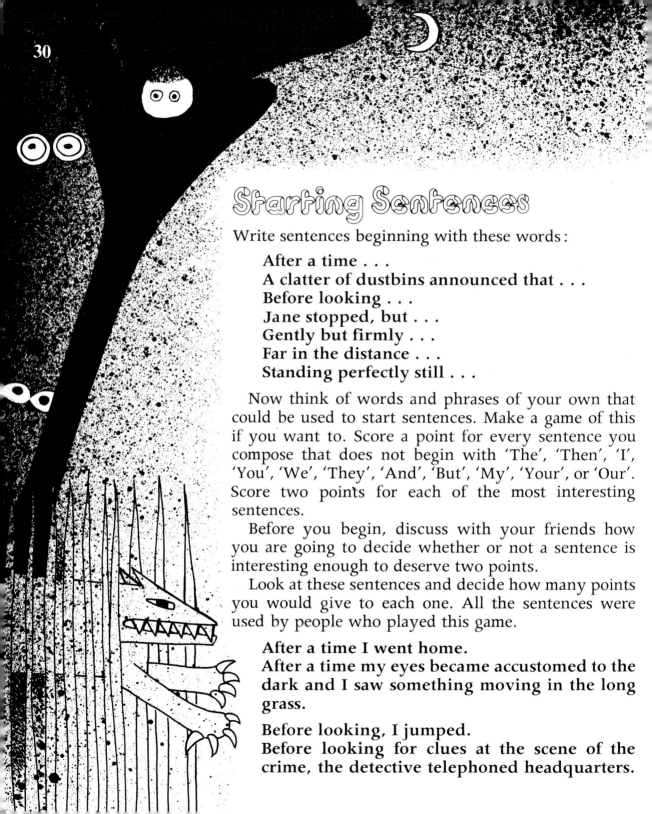

Starting Sentences

Write sentences beginning with these words:

> After a time . . .
> A clatter of dustbins announced that . . .
> Before looking . . .
> Jane stopped, but . . .
> Gently but firmly . . .
> Far in the distance . . .
> Standing perfectly still . . .

Now think of words and phrases of your own that could be used to start sentences. Make a game of this if you want to. Score a point for every sentence you compose that does not begin with 'The', 'Then', 'I', 'You', 'We', 'They', 'And', 'But', 'My', 'Your', or 'Our'. Score two points for each of the most interesting sentences.

Before you begin, discuss with your friends how you are going to decide whether or not a sentence is interesting enough to deserve two points.

Look at these sentences and decide how many points you would give to each one. All the sentences were used by people who played this game.

> After a time I went home.
> After a time my eyes became accustomed to the dark and I saw something moving in the long grass.
>
> Before looking, I jumped.
> Before looking for clues at the scene of the crime, the detective telephoned headquarters.

A Special Event

Try to remember an event or visit that excited you, such as a picnic, a visit to the circus, or an outing, and start to plan an account of what happened that day.

If you wish, you can make your starting-point the moment when you woke up at the beginning of the day. Mention your thoughts and feelings, and remember to begin your sentences in different ways.

Here are the first few words of two sentences. Use other interesting constructions of your own.

After a restless night . . .
Through a gap in the curtains . . .

Another Point of View

It is often fun to look at the world from a completely different angle. Does the world appear the same from the top of a tall building as it does at ground level?

Choose one of the following ideas for a story. Try to see the scene from a different angle, and write about your thoughts as well as about what happens.

Imagine you are a bird perched on the highest point of the school roof, watching everyone come out of school at break-time.

Imagine you are the basket your mother uses when she goes shopping.

Don't begin every sentence with 'I' or 'Then'. Think of other ways to start them, for example:

Perched high on the roof . . .
The children below . . .
When I'm empty, I lie . . .
Swinging gently in Susan's hand . . .

An Exciting Holiday

In a book called *Winter Holiday* by Arthur Ransome, Dick, one of the boys, has to climb along a mountain ledge.

He set foot on the ledge, left the steep, snow-covered slope, and had a sheer drop below him to the rocky screes. But, at first, the ledge was broad enough for easy walking, and he stepped out confidently, every few yards taking hold of the rope and flicking it outwards so that it moved with him along the cliff. Here and there the snow had been blown from the ledge or melted and he could see tufts of grass. Scientifically speaking, of course, it was no harder than walking along a narrow path. But it somehow felt very different when he looked down past his feet to the grey rocks that showed through the snow so far below him.

Do you need to look up any of the words in the passage in your dictionary?

Read the passage again and notice that the sentences are constructed in various ways.

Discuss how the author describes what Dick saw, did and felt.

Think of a time when you were very high up. Talk about what you saw and did, and about your feelings. Then write a story, making your sentences as interesting as you can.

Joining Simple Sentences

If you write several simple sentences one after the other, you will find that the effect is rather jerky. Sometimes you may want to give an effect like this. For example:

> **A shot rang out. Everyone stood still. The robber shouted, ''Lie down!''**

If you do not want to give this effect, you will need to find ways of joining simple sentences together. Look at these sentences:

> **I entered the supermarket. I collected a wire basket. I began to search for the items on my list.**

There are several ways in which the three sentences could be joined. Here is one of them:

> **I entered the supermarket, collected a wire basket and began to search for the items on my list.**

Now join the three sentences together in a different way and use the sentence you make as the starting-point for a story about a visit to a supermarket.

More Groups of Sentences

Here are two other examples of groups of simple sentences which can be joined together to make them read more smoothly:

> **It was raining. Suddenly the sun broke through the clouds. I saw a rainbow. The colours were red, orange, yellow, green, blue, indigo and violet.**

> **I saw a lot of cars. I saw motor cycles. Taxis were speeding along. I saw heavy lorries grinding slowly up the slight hill.**

Think of different ways of joining the sentences in the examples above, or describe one of the scenes in your own words.

How Much Do You Notice?

It is surprising how some people see and notice much more than others.

Detectives looking for clues at the scene of a crime notice many details other people miss. Trackers in forests observe tracks and signs of creatures that other people never see at all.

The Senses Game

How sharp are your senses? Ask your teacher to arrange a quiz. Two teams of four or five people should take turns at trying to guess various items by using only certain of their senses—sight, hearing, smell, taste and touch.

Ask your teacher to test each member of the teams in turn, giving them appropriate instructions. Here are some suggestions for items to guess:

TOUCH, SMELL AND TASTE (eyes closed)
apple, orange, banana, bowl of cornflakes, salt, cheese, biscuit, nut, jam, lemonade, milk, chocolate

TOUCH AND SMELL (eyes closed)
ink, soap, toothpaste, paraffin, disinfectant, perfume

TOUCH ONLY (eyes closed)
screw, hairbrush, stick of chalk, pair of spectacles, egg-cup, leaf, pine-cone

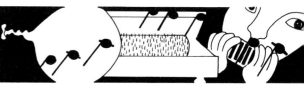

HEARING ONLY (eyes closed)
a balloon being blown up, a musical box, three notes played on a recorder, a pencil being sharpened, a pin being dropped, a door being shut, scissors being used, a coin being tossed, a match being struck, a piece of paper being torn, a chord played on a mouth-organ

SIGHT
pictures of familiar items taken from unusual angles

a poet's point of view

Poets observe people and the world around them very carefully. In poetry they describe their thoughts and feelings about what they see.

Read this poem, 'Long Distance Lorry', by Philip Callow. Notice that there are no rhymes.

Red truck slumbering in the alley
at midday, tucked out of sight;
a wintry sun just missing the tin roof.
The driver and his mate fast asleep,
keeled over sideways, both of them,
as if sleep had hit them from one side.
Strangers. I go by surprised,
staring at them through the windscreen.
Unknowns. I go by unknown,
lingering, nobody in sight.
One is yellow about the face,
the other needs a shave.
Babes in the cab. Secrets
and journeys on their eyelids,
their faces bathed with tiredness.
I shall never see them again.

Now write a verse of your own about someone you have seen and looked at carefully, but may never see again.

Observing and Recording

Test Your Powers of Observation

Here is a simple test. See how well you notice and remember details of your everyday life.

1 Describe yesterday's weather. (Mention any wind or rain, the sun, the sky and the temperature.)
2 Which daily newspaper do you have at home?
3 If you read the newspaper, describe a news item that you remember. Tell the story and say approximately when the events took place.
4 Give the day and time of a television programme you enjoy.
5 Describe, as accurately as you can, the colour and pattern of the curtains in a room at home.
6 Give an account of an item mentioned in school assembly today.
7 Describe what you did last Saturday morning. Did you enjoy yourself?
8 Think of the last time you cried, or laughed uproariously. What made you cry or laugh?

Here are some things which you may find interesting to do. Observe what takes place in each experiment and then write an account of how you feel and what you see.

Collect several pieces of differently-coloured cellophane. Look through the cellophane at the things and people around you. What would you think and what would your feelings be if the world changed colour overnight? Write about it.

Find out the meanings of these words, which you may be able to use in describing what you saw:

transparent   monochrome
suffused light   harmony

Oil and Water

Here is another experiment with colour.

You will need a bowl of water, some ink and some oil. Darken the water in the bowl by putting ink in it. Then drop several blobs of oil on to the water. Take the bowl into the light and watch what happens. Describe what you see. These words may help you. Find their meanings in a dictionary.

contrast reflected blend
brilliant shades   hues

These are the colours of the rainbow:

red, orange, yellow, green, blue, indigo, violet.

Collect and label pieces of paper or cloth of each of these colours. Look again carefully at the colours of the oil pattern floating on the water and see if you can identify each colour of the rainbow. Write several sentences explaining what you did and what you saw.

Make a collage by cutting attractive shapes from the paper or material, grouping them together and gluing them on to a card.

A Candle in the Dark

Here is a simple situation which you could use as the starting-point for a story.

Ask your teacher to supervise this experiment.

You will need a candle, a saucer and a box of matches.

Stand the candle on a saucer in the middle of a table and sit round the table with a group of friends. Ask your teacher to light the candle. Then watch the flame, the wax of the candle, the shadows and the faces of your friends.

There will be a particularly good effect if the lighted candle is placed safely in a small, dark room, such as a store-room, where any windows can be blacked out.

Afterwards, talk about what you observed.

Find words that describe your feelings as you watched. Look up these words in a dictionary:

illuminate   **radiate**
flicker   **grotesque**

Now think of the situation as the starting-point of a story.

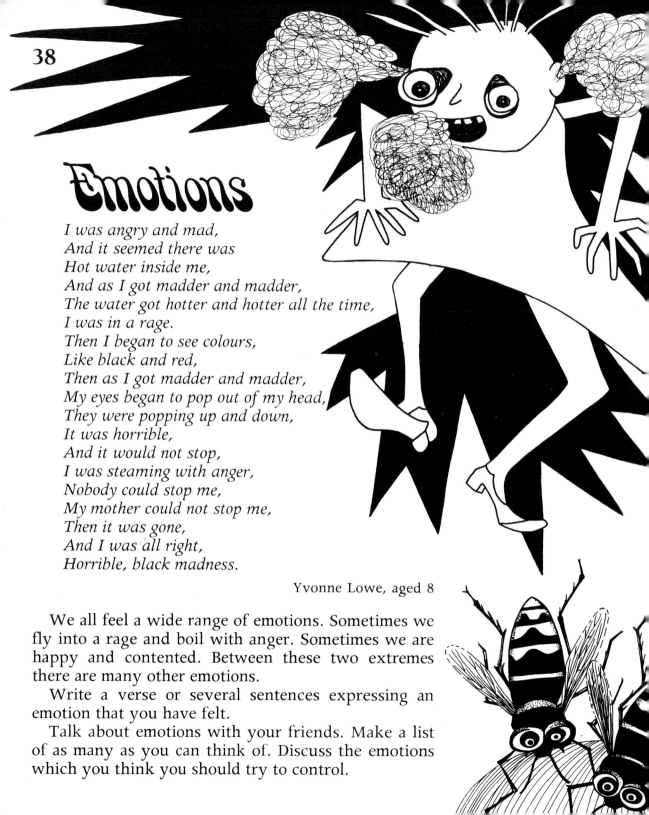

Emotions

I was angry and mad,
And it seemed there was
Hot water inside me,
And as I got madder and madder,
The water got hotter and hotter all the time,
I was in a rage.
Then I began to see colours,
Like black and red,
Then as I got madder and madder,
My eyes began to pop out of my head,
They were popping up and down,
It was horrible,
And it would not stop,
I was steaming with anger,
Nobody could stop me,
My mother could not stop me,
Then it was gone,
And I was all right,
Horrible, black madness.

Yvonne Lowe, aged 8

We all feel a wide range of emotions. Sometimes we fly into a rage and boil with anger. Sometimes we are happy and contented. Between these two extremes there are many other emotions.

Write a verse or several sentences expressing an emotion that you have felt.

Talk about emotions with your friends. Make a list of as many as you can think of. Discuss the emotions which you think you should try to control.

Situations to Mime

Imagine yourself in each of the situations described below and think how you would feel. Then try to mime each incident.

FEAR
A tiger has escaped from a zoo and is roaming the streets. Unaware of the danger, you are walking cheerfully along the street. Then you turn a corner and there, in front of you, is a full-grown tiger!

SURPRISE AND PLEASURE
You are on your own and miserable because you have no one to play with. Unexpectedly, your aunt calls in to invite you to the zoo.

SORROW
A motor car has stopped and a small group of children has gathered around something lying at the side of the road. You push through the little group and see your pet, lying in the gutter.

PANIC
Two wasps are buzzing around your head as you read a book.

Now choose one of the incidents and write about it. How did you feel? What happened?

In Your Own Experience

Think of times when you have had strong feelings, and write about one particular incident. Here are some titles that you may like to consider:

Finally I lost my temper   **A selfish person**
I couldn't stop laughing   **A sad moment**

Criticism

With some friends, discuss things that you don't like.
Here are some subjects that may start you thinking:

food	people
colours	places
clothes	seasons, weather
sounds	things that have to be done

In your discussion, explain why you don't like a
particular thing and why you prefer something else.

Write several sentences about 'One thing I don't
like'.

Your Own Work

You probably find it very easy to talk about things you
don't like. Most people have no difficulty in criticising
(saying what they think is wrong with) other people
and things they see. But many people find it much more
difficult to criticise themselves and their own work.

Try it yourself! Look at a piece of written work that
you have done recently. Read it carefully and criticise
it. Ask yourself:

1 Is the meaning clear?
2 Is it a lively piece of writing?
3 Have I written interesting sentences?
4 Have I begun each sentence with a capital
   letter?
5 Does each sentence finish with a full stop?
6 How could I improve this piece of work?

A Friend's Work

When you have read your own work and criticised it, show it to a friend. Read and criticise each other's work. Don't forget that a critic looks for good points as well as bad. Ask each other questions about what you read.

Someone Else's Work

Look at the pictures on this page and criticise the work of the artists who painted them.

Right and Wrong

Your opinions and criticisms are more likely to be sound and sensible when you decide what is right and wrong, what is good and bad and what is true and false.

Try to do this as you discuss the following subjects with your friends. Then choose one and write about it.

It's a very bad habit
Some of my good habits
What I'm not allowed to do at home

top: Da Vinci, *The Virgin of the Rocks* left: Uccello, *The Battle of San Romano* above: Constable, *Salisbury Cathedral* below: H. Rousseau, *Tiger in a Storm*

Spare Time

How do you spend your spare time? With your friends, discuss what you do. Then write about your favourite pastimes and draw pictures to illustrate your writing.

An Autobiography

When H. E. Bates wrote his autobiography (the story of his life), he recalled the games he had played as a young boy. He had clear ideas in his mind. Read the passage below and see if he has succeeded in putting his ideas clearly into words. After reading the passage for the first time, go back to the beginning and guess the meanings of words that you do not know. Then look them up in your dictionary.

So fortified, in my case by hot tea, hot toast spread with home-made lard and salt—and how very good it was—we all went out on early winter evenings, to the gas-lit street stage. I remember the winter evenings more vividly, I suppose, than the summer ones simply because of the gas-light, the one big street light round which we played

Sally go round the Moon
Sally go round the Stars
Sally go round the Chimney pot
On a Sunday afternoon.

and the lights in three shops.

Almost always, I think, we first gathered round the window of one of the bakers' shops to sort out the preliminaries for play. Certain preliminaries had to be gone through, among them the picking of teams, and also 'who was going to start it'. We always did this by rhymes. Thus, as we gathered in a circle, one of us went round, pointing to each in turn, reciting:

Paddy on the railway, picking up
  hard stones
Down came the engine and broke
  Paddy's bones.
"Well," said Paddy, "that isn't
  fair."
"Well," said the engine, "I don't
  care."
O-U-T spells
Out goes she.

After this the teams divided up, one going to the far side of the street, the other remaining by the shop windows, so to speak, on home ground.

Reading

Read what you have written about your favourite pastimes and then read again what H. E. Bates wrote. Say what your plan was and what you think was the plan used by H. E. Bates.

In the Past

Have you ever listened to your mother, father or uncle telling the story of something that happened when they were young? Most of us are fascinated by such stories, because they are about real people and things.

Tell your friends the story of something that happened to someone you know, or to someone in history. Make a plan before you begin.

As you tell your story, try to describe the person's thoughts and feelings as well as other details of what happened.

FICTION

Most of the stories we read are not true. They have been created in the minds of authors. But the people, places and incidents are true to life and seem real to us.

You have probably imagined yourself having adventures on a desert island in the tropics. Clive Dalton has written several tropical island adventure stories. In the book, *Malay Schooner*, he tells how three boys, Richard, Kitchie and Wong, suddenly see a schooner drifting towards their island.

The three boys lay face downwards, elbows in the sand, chins held in their cupped hands, and watched the three small boats they had made. They were not really boats; just the husks of coconuts, cut into segments, with pieces of wood stuck into the soft fibre to form masts, and squares of broad plantain leaf for sails.

It was one of their favourite games to make these little boats, launch them in the shallows and race them against each other . . .

Richard, shifting his position to make himself more comfortable, raised his eyes and looked around. There was seldom much to be seen in the near-by seascape, except an occasional passing junk or a very distant liner. Nothing ever approached the island itself.

It was, therefore, with astonishment that Richard now saw a sail some little way off. He stared at it almost unbelievingly for a few moments and then pointed it out to the other two.

"Look at that!"

The other two looked up and stared at the approaching sail. It seemed to be making straight for the island.

"It's coming here," said Kitchie incredulously.

"It looks like it," agreed Richard, "but why?"

As it came nearer they saw that the sail was old and patched. It was faded brown, but down one side was a streak of equally faded blue, and right in the centre was an oblong of grubby white.

The breeze was not very strong and the sail flapped limply against the mast, puffing out occasionally to give the ship a little headway.

"It doesn't look as though there's anyone aboard," Richard said.

In a few paragraphs the scene is set for the beginning of an adventure story. I wonder what happened next? You could read the book and find out. But do you think you could write the story of the adventures of Richard, Kitchie and Wong yourself? Plan the adventure they had with the schooner that drifted to their island, and then write out your story.

If this idea does not appeal to you, then choose one of the titles below for a story. Make a plan before you start to write.

Mountain rescue   **Fog-bound**
Saved by helicopter   **Forced landing**

Back to the Beginning

This book began by giving the purpose of speech and writing as follows:

The final cause of speech and writing is to get an idea, as exactly as possible, out of one mind into another.

The best way to do this is in stages. Here are the most important of these:

1 **thinking** (until the idea is clear in your mind)
2 **planning** (making notes so that the parts of the idea are in the right order)
3 **choosing** (selecting parts of the idea to be made into sentences)
4 **writing or speaking** (using words that express your thoughts and feelings as clearly as possible).

Speech

Keeping the four stages in your mind, prepare a talk to give to a group of friends or to your class. See if you can talk clearly on the subject you choose for about two or three minutes.

Here are some suggestions:

I'm glad I don't have to decide . . .
The kind of person I am
When I'm eighteen . . .
Something really interesting . . .

Writing

Here are some subjects to write about:

dogs, whales, lions, giraffes
(or any other kinds of creatures)
waterfalls, caves, springs
(or any other natural features)
My hobby
A scene I shall never forget
A secret hide-out
Footprints in the sand
Lost in a forest
Narrow escape
Thin ice
A race for life
Shipwreck
A visit to the dentist
A dream (pleasant or frightening)
My ambition
A holiday

Choose one topic and write about it. Don't forget the four stages:

1 Think   3 Plan

2 Choose   4 Write